THE FURIES

MONSTERS OF MYTHOLOGY

25 VOLUMES

Hellenic

Amycus
Anteus
The Calydonian Boar
Cerberus
Chimaera
The Cyclopes
The Dragon of Boeotia
The Furies
Geryon
Harpalyce
Hecate
The Hydra
Ladon
Medusa
The Minotaur
The Nemean Lion
Procrustes
Scylla and Charybdis
The Sirens
The Spear-birds
The Sphinx

Norse

Fafnir
Fenris

Celtic

Drabne of Dole
Pig's Ploughman

MONSTERS OF MYTHOLOGY

THE FURIES

Bernard Evslin

CHELSEA HOUSE PUBLISHERS

New York   Philadelphia

1989

EDITOR
Remmel Nunn

ART DIRECTOR
Maria Epes

PICTURE RESEARCHER
Susan Quist

SENIOR DESIGNER
Marjorie Zaum

EDITORIAL ASSISTANTS
Nate Eaton, Heather Lewis, Mark Rifkin

5   7   9   8   6   4

Library of Congress Cataloging-in-Publication Data

Evslin, Bernard.
The furies.

(Monsters of mythology)
Summary: A retelling of the myths associated with the
terrible goddesses of vengeance who lived in Hades and
punished people for every kind of crime.
1. Erinyes (Greek mythology)—Juvenile literature.
[1. Erinyes (Greek mythology) 2. Mythology, Greek]
I. Title. II. Series: Evslin, Bernard. Monsters of mythology.
BL820.F8E96   1989   398.21'0938
89-7334

ISBN 0-55546-249-9

Printed and bound in Mexico.

For MARY EVSLIN
whose sorceries humanize bears

Characters

Monsters

The Furies Three flying hags who serve Hades: Alecto (uh LECK toh), the Strange One; Megaera (meh JEE rah), Dark Memory; and Tisiphone (ti SIFF oh nee), Vengeance

Gods

Uranus
(YOOR uh nuhs) The rain god, first King of Heaven, and Father of the Gods

Cronos
(KROH nuhs) Titan son of Uranus, second King of the Gods

Rhea
(REE ah) Wife of Cronos, mother of Zeus, earth goddess

Zeus
(ZOOS) Last King of the Gods

Hera
(HEE ruh) Wife of Zeus, Queen of the Gods

Hades
(HAY deez) Brother of Zeus, Ruler of the Dead

Poseidon (poh SY duhn)	Another brother of Zeus, God of the Sea
Athena (uh THEE nuh)	Daughter of Zeus, Goddess of Wisdom
Apollo (uh PAHL oh)	Son of Zeus, new solar deity
Helios (HEE lih ohs)	A Titan, first sun god
Dione (dy OH nee)	Former oak goddess
Circe (SUR see)	Daughter of Helios, demigoddess

Mortals

Shepherd, shepherdess	Guardians of the infant Zeus
Little Husband	Husband of Dione
Salmoneus (sal MOH nee uhs)	King of Aeolis, who pretends to be a god
Hairy Man	Bandit of Argos
Ulysses (u LISS eez)	Greek war chief, King of Ithaca

BOOKS BY BERNARD EVSLIN

Merchants of Venus
Heroes, Gods and Monsters of the Greek Myths
Greeks Bearing Gifts: The Epics of Achilles and Ulysses
The Dolphin Rider
Gods, Demigods and Demons
The Green Hero
Heraclea
Signs & Wonders: Tales of the Old Testament

Contents

1

Trouble in Heaven

elios was the first sun driver, a Titan who guided the fire-maned stallions as they pulled the golden chariot east to west across the blue meadow of the sky, casting daylight on the earth below.

Now, Cronos and his court Titans were all very vain and haughty, quick to anger and slow to forgive, but Helios, who dwelt amid flame, had the hottest temper of all.

Down on earth, that new race of creature called *human*—who understood nothing yet but were amazed and awed by every-thing—stared in wonder at the daily miracle of the enormous black sky growing pale, then flushing pink. Joy flowered in them as they watched darkness being scattered by sheaves of light. They watched as a golden disk of light trundled over the sky, allowing them to see again, making them warm again. Although informed by nothing but the light itself, they knew that they were seeing one wheel of a great fire chariot called the Sun, and that its charioteer was a god named Helios.

And so the first prayers of mankind were raised not to Cronos, King of the Gods, but to Helios, the only god they saw, the only one they knew about. And Helios was pleased by these songs of praise rising from earth and by the stone altars loaded with fruit and flowers and joints of meat—all for him.

"Ho ho!" he chortled to himself. "Cronos may call himself king and strut about Olympus telling us what to do and who is to do it, but it's me man worships. Me, me, me!"

So he was very happy in his work. He loved his great sleek fire-maned stallions, loved the golden chariot and his daily ride over the sky, watching the new-made earth and its jeweled seas unreeling beneath him. Riding high, he was able to pick out the most beautiful of the nymphs who dwelt on mountain slope, wood, and stream. Often, he would dive out of his chariot and chase one of them, knowing that his sun stallions would trot about in slow circles until he flew up to the chariot again.

Once or twice, however, it happened that he spent so much time with a nymph that his horses dipped low to search for him, firing the earth and leaving great scorched places that were later called deserts. And nobody knew how these places came to be until long afterward. Once, while Helios was chasing an oread,

Helios loved his great sleek fire-maned stallions,
loved the golden chariot
and his daily ride over the sky.

or mountain nymph, the horses circled the same peak until it melted inside, blowing its top, spitting flame and red-hot rock. And so, it is told, were volcanoes born.

Uranus, whose name means "rain," was the First One, Ruler of Sky and Earth and the new boiling seas—and All Above, Beyond, and Between. He ruled wisely and well, and the lesser gods expected him to be king forever, but his son Cronos thought otherwise. Cronos was loud in admiration of his father, pretended utter devotion, and kept singing his praises up to the time that he murdered him.

Actually, murder isn't the right word. Gods are immortal. They can be surprised and dismembered by other gods; even so, each piece will hold a life of its own. But Cronos was as cunning as he was cruel. He had the great body of his father chopped into a thousand bloody gobbets and scattered them over the entire surface of the earth and dropped them into every sea.

Then Cronos announced that because of the tragic and mysterious disappearance of the mighty Uranus, he, Cronos, eldest son, would take the throne until his father chose to reappear. Everyone knew what had happened, if not exactly how, and knew that Uranus would never reappear. But they all feared Cronos and vowed to serve him faithfully.

So Cronos proclaimed himself king, put on the star-encrusted crown and the gorgeous cloud-wool Judgment Cloak, dyed in all the colors of the sunset, and began his reign. He imposed a stricter order upon the wild new earth and divided the work of controlling nature among the Titans, who were his brothers and sisters. It was at that time that he awarded Helios the important task of driving the sun chariot.

Although Cronos held absolute and unchallenged power, he was familiar with fear. For he was haunted by a certain memory, which, instead of fading, seemed to grow more vivid as time passed. The memory was of himself holding a bloody sword as he watched his father's head tumbling in the dust. But the head stopped rolling—stood on its stump of a neck and spoke:

*The head stopped rolling—
stood on its stump of a
neck and spoke.*

"O Son, you kill me now and steal my throne. But what you have done to me shall be done to you—by a child of your own."

Cronos had great mastery over himself. During the day he was able to shut out this memory. But at night the head floated into his sleep, looking at him out of scooped and empty eyes. In the white thicket of its beard a black hole opened, speaking those same words:

"What has been done to me shall be done to you—by a child of your own . . ."

For three nights in a row the head visited his sleep. On the third night Cronos answered: "No! It shall not be! No child of mine shall slay me. It won't live long enough."

The hundred-headed giant who guarded the royal bedchamber heard his master utter a strangled shout, and ran in to defend him, each hand wielding a tree-trunk club. Cronos awoke and saw the gigantic figure looming above him. He sprang out of bed.

"What do you want?" he growled.

"Pardon, My Lord," said the giant. "I heard you call. You must have had a bad dream."

"Very bad," said Cronos. "But it taught me what to do."

Now Cronos's young wife, Rhea, was bursting with her first child and happily awaiting its appearance. Cronos surprised her by showing great concern. He would attend the birth, he insisted, to make sure everything went well.

It was a hard labor. Rhea swooned briefly, and swam back to consciousness holding out her arms for her infant. No baby came into her arms, nor did she see any midwife—just her husband looking sadly down at her.

"Where's my baby?" she whispered. "Is it a boy or girl? Give it to me, give it to me."

"Oh, Wife," said Cronos with a half sob. "I regret to tell you that our child was born dead. I've already buried it to spare you pain."

"Your mouth is all bloody," she whispered.

Hastily, he wiped the blood away with the back of his hand. "In my anguish I must have bitten my lips," he said. "Do not grieve, dear wife. We'll have other children, many more."

"Oh, yes," she murmured.

"I'll have to be more careful next time," he said to himself. For what had happened was that to destroy all evidence he had eaten the baby.

Three vanished babies later Rhea began to get suspicious. She also got pregnant again. And when her fifth baby disappeared in the same way, her suspicion grew into a furious certainty, for now she realized that her husband had swallowed all their children and meant to keep doing so. But she was determined that he would not.

When she was again ripe with child and felt her time coming she sneaked out of the palace, down the slope of Olympus, and into a dark wood. There, beneath a great oak, she delivered her own child—a boy. She slung a cradle of vines in the tree, suckled him, and put him to sleep. Then she found a rock the right size, wrapped it in swaddling clothes, climbed the mountain and entered the royal bedchamber, holding the rock to her breast and humming a lullaby.

Snorting and bellowing, Cronos arose from his great bed. He snatched the bundle from her and swallowed it, clothes and all—and was amazed. The five other children he had swallowed had given him no trouble at all. This one lay like a stone on his stomach.

Rhea sympathized very sweetly when he complained of indigestion, and, indeed, was all laughter inside. She stole down the mountain again and took her boy from the vine cradle. She found an honest shepherd family and gave them the babe to raise, promising them a great crop of lambs each spring, and a huge hound that would protect their flock from wolves.

The child's name was Zeus, she told them; he was the son of a king and would be a mighty king himself.

"Oh, yes, yes!" cried the shepherd's wife. "Look at him shining there in the manger. He makes the straw look like gold. Not a prince he seems, but a young god."

And Rhea's heart sang as she made her way up the mountain again. She knew her precious babe would be safe with that family until such time as she could fetch him again.

So the secret was kept. Cronos did not know that he had swallowed a rock instead of an infant, and that the dangerous babe, quite uneaten, was out in the world growing fast. Indeed, Zeus was no longer a baby but a boy. And the boy was growing into a glorious youth. Gray-eyed, suavely powerful, with a joyous, bawling voice and a smile that could melt snow, he prowled the slope like a young panther. So splendid a creature had he

*Rhea found an honest shepherd family
and gave them the babe to raise,
promising them a great crop
of lambs each spring.*

become that he amazed even his doting mother, and she realized that his divinity could not be concealed much longer.

And one night she smuggled him into the cloud castle atop Olympus.

The next morning she sought out Cronos and said: "I have a surprise for you, my dear."

"Do you?" he growled. "I'm not sure I like surprises. In fact, I'm sure I don't."

"Oh, you'll like this one. I've engaged a new cupbearer."

"Why? What happened to the old one?"

"*You* happened to him, My Lord. Don't you recall? You split his skull with your scepter when he splashed some wine on your sleeve. Surely, you remember. It was just last week."

"Oh, that . . . Did I really hit him hard or is the rascal just pretending?"

"I don't know, dear, but he isn't here anymore. I don't

know whether the brains spilled out of that crack in his head or he simply decided it was healthier to vanish. But we need a new cupbearer. And I've found one."

"Who?"

"I think you'll like him. He's a cousin from a far-off place. Son of bickering Titans whose quarrels grew so violent that their children all ran away. This lad sought refuge here on Olympus. And knowing how you like handsome servants, I took him on immediately. He's a real beauty. You'll see."

Cronos saw and approved. And Zeus stayed on at the Castle of the Gods, serving as cupbearer. When Cronos was away, he and his mother walked in the garden, weaving a plot. Now, in the manner of gods, when they decided what to do they began to do it. In the midnight kitchen they brewed a strong potion—mustard and stump water, to which was added a paste of crushed fire ants. They let it steep for two days.

"I don't know, Mother," said Zeus. "See how it hisses and foams? Surely he'll notice it, and know there's something wrong."

"Perhaps not," said Rhea. "I'll have the cook prepare his favorite dish—pig's heart and calf brains. He'll hurl himself on the food very greedily, and when he eats, he drinks. Perhaps he'll gulp the brew down without suspecting anything."

"Well," said Zeus, "we always knew it would be a risky business. But it's worth it."

At noon on the third day Zeus filled his father's golden goblet with the special drink. Rhea had ordered the cook to oversalt the pig's heart and calf brains, and when Cronos had devoured a huge serving he was very thirsty. He snatched up the hissing goblet and drained it in a single gulp.

He arose from his chair, retching and gasping. He vomited up first a stone, then all the children he had swallowed—Hestia, Demeter, Hera, Hades, and Poseidon, who, being gods, were still undigested, still alive. At the first touch of sunlight they grew to full size, and stood forth in the glory of their prime. They

A son of Zeus named Apollo became Lord of the Golden Bow, sun god, and charioteer.

greeted their mother and their brother with loud cries of joy and clustered about Zeus, praising him and embracing him—and immediately chose him to be their leader. But when they turned to rend their father, they found that he had slipped away.

But Cronos soon made himself felt again. He called his Titans to arms; he summoned his Giants and a flight of fire-spitting dragons, and led this fearsome array against the young gods.

But Zeus had won the loyalty of the Cyclopes, gigantic one-eyed creatures who were the world's first weapon makers. And Cronos had so mistreated the lesser gods, woodland deities, and those of river and field, that they, too, came to fight under Zeus. Thus began the War of the Gods, a series of battles that raged across the floor of heaven, shaking earth and sea, spawning bloody tales and terrifying mankind so badly that human dreams were colored by terror to the end of time. But for this tale all we need to know is that the younger gods won the final battle. Cronos and his Titans were forced to flee, and Zeus ruled as King of Heaven.

Whereupon he divided all powers among his brothers and sisters, his sons and daughters. Helios, the huge, shaggy, flame-haired charioteer, was barred from his golden coach and forbidden even to say farewell to his beloved sun stallions. And a son of Zeus named Apollo became Lord of the Golden Bow, sun god, and charioteer.

2

The Furies

eus, as King of the Gods, sometimes visited the realms ruled by his brothers. For the sea god, Poseidon, and Hades, Lord of the Dead, had to be watched closely lest they steal some of his powers.

Both of his brothers received Zeus with great courtesy and sought to lull his suspicions by overwhelming him with hospitality. Poseidon heaped magnificent gifts upon him—spear, sword, and dagger of polished walrus ivory, a bib of first-water pearls, and armlets of gold taken from the holds of sunken treasure ships—and served up a braid of the most gorgeous sea nymphs to attend him wherever he went.

Hades entertained Zeus with strange spectacles. He demonstrated his entire stock of tortures—the Great Mangle, the Marrow-log, the Spiked Shirt—and took him on a tour of the roasting pits.

Now, the shades that inhabit Death's domain are just that—shades, ghosts. They have shed their bodies, leaving pinkish white vapors that drift over the scorched plains of Erebus. But any shade who has been sentenced to torment is clothed again in flesh so that it may again know pain.

And Zeus watched as the condemned shades suffered the attentions of harpies, pitchfork fiends, and assorted demons. He turned every once in a while to praise his brother's ingenuity and the efficiency of his staff, but vowed to himself to send someone else on the next inspection trip. Like all the gods, Zeus could be very cruel when angered, but the spectacle of so much pain when he felt no wrath just made him gloomy. But his interest was quickened when Hades ordered the Furies into action.

Who were these Furies?

They were three hags, sisters, related to the Harpies but even more horrid. They, too, wore brass wings and brass claws and wielded stingray whips, but they were larger than the Harpies, totally vicious, and were used to torment those who had especially displeased Hades. Their Greek names—Tisiphone, Alecto, and Megaera—meant Vengeance, Strange One, and Dark Memory, but they called each other Tiss, Ally, and Meg.

"Watch this!" cried Hades. He pointed to a section of scorched field where iron racks sprouted like trees, and their branches bore leather loops instead of leaves. In a clearing before this weird grove huddled newly fleshed shades. Hades whistled.

Zeus stared as three brass-winged hags dived separately upon three condemned shades, who resembled pinkish, plump men. Each hag seized a man and dug her brass claws into the soft places of his body, so that the victims began to scream before their official punishment started. Tiss flew to a rack, folded her man over a metal arm and bound him fast. Ally and Meg flew to separate racks and tethered their men in the same way. They wheeled then, and, standing on air, curtsied to Hades.

The Lord of the Dead sliced his hand through the air. The three Furies wheeled again, unslung the stingray whips from their girdles, and made the barbed lashes whistle through the air as they began to flog the three pink men. Now arose a screaming and sobbing such as Zeus had never heard before. He sat like a rock. The screaming turned to choked, phlegmy howls. Zeus frowned. It had all become unpleasant to him.

Three brass-winged hags dived separately
upon three condemned shades,
who resembled pinkish, plump men.

The sounds stopped as suddenly as they had begun. Silence lay upon the scorched plain. Every scrap of flesh had been flayed from the condemned; only bloody, pulsing gobs clung to the metal branches. They were shades again. But pain had been branded so deeply into their cores that they would never stop suffering, even though they had lost their torn flesh.

The Furies coiled their whips. They flew toward the ebony throne, circled Hades once in a flurry of black robes, and flew off into the mist.

"Interesting," said Zeus. "Are they what you call the Furies?"

"They are."

"You know," said Zeus, "I'm glad I came down here. You've given me some interesting ideas."

"Me? Furnish ideas to the worlds's central intellect?" murmured Hades. "You overpraise me, My Lord."

"Your modesty is becoming," said Zeus. "But unconvincing. I know you know how clever you are.'

"And what idea have I given you?"

"And what idea have I given you?" asked Hades.

"I admire the way you keep your unruly shades in order. It is difficult, I know, to frighten a ghost. But your staff seems to spread a great deal of wholesome terror, particularly the Furies."

"Yes," said Hades. "They are specially bred, specially trained, and I reserve them for special occasions."

"I have special cases, too," said Zeus. "And they're increasing. The human herd grows more restive as it matures. Some of my mortals are quite untamable."

"They break your laws?"

"Oh, yes, every day—and particularly at night."

"But do they not fear the suffering that will be inflicted upon them after death? Surely they must be aware of the torments I have to offer."

"You know, Brother," said Zeus, "I'm afraid that mortals don't really believe in death. Very few of them actually think they're going to die. They see others die, of course, but every man seems to think that he will somehow prove to be the one solitary exception—most women, too. So the idea of after-death torments doesn't really keep them in line. What I need to do is punish them more vigorously *before* death."

"Of course, of course!" cried Hades. "That is just what you must do."

"Which leads me to a favor I'm about to ask you," said Zeus. "May I borrow your Furies sometime?"

"But certainly . . . anytime," muttered Hades, trying to smile but not quite succeeding. He hated to give away anything, and lending something to Zeus, he knew, meant *giving* it if the King of the Gods decided that he liked what had been lent.

Zeus read Hades' uneasiness and laughed to himself. It was not easy to embarrass his haughty brother; it was something to be relished whenever he did.

"I thank you in advance," he boomed genially. "And thank you again for all your hospitality. Now, farewell."

3

The Angry Titan

Everything about Helios was violent. When he was told that he could no longer drive the golden chariot, his violent love for the sun turned to violent hatred. He loathed the light and sought the dark.

He found a burned-out crater, scooped out tons of dead ash and rearranged mighty boulders, roofing the crater, making a fortress of the hollow mountain. No windows, no arrow slits, no way for light to get in, just a swiveling slab of rock to serve as a portal. And there he dwelt, coming out only at night, for he did not wish to see the sun being driven by someone else. He came out, in fact, only on moonless nights, because Artemis, twin sister of Apollo, was the moon goddess, and he hated her, too.

When he was abroad on such nights he prowled the slopes, quenching light whenever it appeared, even a glimmer. A traveler, once, lost his way and found himself riding his donkey up an unfamiliar path. He raised his pine-knot torch to see where he was. It was immediately knocked away, and he felt himself rising into the air. An awful, unseen force lifted animal and rider and hurled them off the mountain. The donkey was killed, but the rider lived to tell his tale. And when the story stopped spreading, everyone in the countryside knew that an ogre prowled that crater, and no one would come near it, especially at night.

Since Helios knew that no traveler would come within miles of his mountain, he was amazed, one moonless night, to see another torch flaring. He rushed toward the spot, but the light was restless; it seemed to be floating, swaying, rising—seemed now to lodge in the branches of a tree. Its color was strange also, not a ruddy red and yellow like pine-knot flame, nor did it cast the strong odor of burning pitch. This light was silvery gold, rather like the color of the moon when it was climbing, and the scent it cast was of violets after a rain. He stood under the tree and looked up, and was amazed at what he saw.

A child straddled the swaying branch, riding it as if it were a horse. Her flying hair did not reflect light; it was a source of light. Each strand was a tendril of pale flame. And it was this pearly fire that allowed him to see her and the branch that she was riding.

With a roar of fury he seized the branch, broke it off and held it aloft, preparing to smash it down on the ground. The little girl clung to it like a monkey, screeching with glee. He stared at her in disbelief; he couldn't understand why she wasn't terrified. And his disbelief changed to stupefied wonder as she slid down the branch and perched on his shoulder, clutching his beard to steady herself.

"Who are you?" he muttered.

"Your daughter."

"I have no daughter."

"Yes. Me."

"Who's your mother?"

"Arlawanda."

"An oread?"

"Dryad."

"I don't remember her."

"She remembers you. Every morning we'd look up at the sky and she'd say, 'There's your father driving the sun chariot.' That's why I'm here. I want you to take me for a ride across the sky."

He roared again. She giggled. "Why are you yelling?" she asked.

"You're as stupid as your mother, whom I'm beginning to remember now."

Her hair did not reflect light;
it was a source of light.
Each strand was a tendril
of pale flame.

"I'm not stupid. Neither is she."

"It's that foul Apollo who drives the sun chariot now, little fool. Not me at all."

"Oh, my, I'm sorry . . ."

"You'll be sorrier if you don't get off my shoulder."

She didn't answer, just tightened her grip on his beard.

"Vanish!" he growled. "Before I do dreadful things to you."

"You won't. I'm your daughter."

"You taint my darkness with your damned bright hair."

"Mother says it's just like yours—except not quite so red."

"My hair and beard are black, can't you see?"

"You just dyed them, that's all. The stuff's coming off on my hand. Why did you do that to yourself? So you wouldn't glow in the dark?"

"That's right. I hate the light. I need utter darkness. Now run away. Get off my mountain while you're still in one piece."

"You won't hurt me. I'm your daughter. You have to love me."

"Love . . . Pah!"

"I don't care whether you drive the sun or not. I've decided to live with you for a while."

He laughed a laugh that was like a snarl.

"Why are you so grumpy?" she asked. "Are you hungry?"

"I'm always hungry."

"Do you do your own cooking?"

"I don't do any cooking. You need a fire to cook with. Fires cast light. I eat my meat raw."

"You can't like it that way."

"I like fires less."

"Well," she said, "I can be quite useful to you. I can cook without fire."

"I take it back," he said. "You're not stupid. You're crazy. Now jump down and disappear. I'm getting very angry."

She did leap off his shoulder, landing lightly as a leaf. "Watch!" she called. She whirled about three times, hair whipping her face like tendrils of flame. She pointed at a rock. "Watch, watch . . ."

Helios saw the rock begin to change shape. Smoke came off it, and a hot meaty smell. He walked slowly toward it.

"It's all right," she said. "It's roast lamb. Eat some."

He tore off a chunk and crammed it into his mouth. It was the most delicious thing he had ever tasted, roasted rare, redolent of garlic, rosemary, and thyme.

"Like it?" she called.

"Not bad," he mumbled. "How'd you do that?"

"I'm quite magical for my age. I can do other things, too. I can be useful to you."

"The most useful thing you can do is go away," he said.

He left her then and entered his cave, plunging again into utter darkness. He thought he heard her voice even through the thick rock and couldn't tell whether she was weeping or singing. Then he heard a crack of thunder and a great wash of rain. He knew that she was still on the slope, waiting for him to come out. He pictured her under a drench of rain. He groaned aloud and stamped his foot so hard he thought he felt the floor of the cave shaking. Like a flower she was crouching under the rain, being nourished by it, growing like a flower in his mind.

He rushed out of the cave. He didn't see her. Wind drove the rain in sheets. He was immediately as wet as though he had jumped into a river. He knew that the black dye was washing out of his hair and beard. He saw the hair of his arms smouldering in the rain. He saw a smaller patch of light.

It streaked up to him and a weight hit him on the chest. Wet arms were about his neck. He smelled violets. "Father, father," she cried. "You came out again! It's raining very hard."

"You don't say," he grunted.

He carried her into the crater. They lit up the darkness. He watched, amazed, as the solid blackness trembled and flowed away from their forms like an ebbing tide. Shocked by light, a canopy of lizards swayed and chittered.

"Lizards!" she caroled. "How lovely!"

"You like them?"

"Oh, yes. Don't you?"

*He thought he heard her voice even through
the thick rock and couldn't tell
whether she was weeping or singing.*

Echo (Number 25, 1951) by Jackson Pollock

He grunted. She laughed and grunted, imitating him. "Does that sound mean yes or no? Never mind, it doesn't matter. What a big cave. What a wonderful place to live. Are you hungry again? Shall I cook something else? Rain makes me very hungry. Doesn't it you?"

"Everything makes me hungry."

After three days the crater was brimming with light. Helios was scrubbed clean. Every hair of his head and beard and body pelt was a glowing filament. The light he cast was the hot red and gold of the sun at noon. And Circe shed a silvery gold, the new quivering light of dawn. Savors of food hung upon the air— baking bread and roasting meat, garlic, rosemary, and thyme.

The exiled Titan, who had been existing in a cold, sullen, clench of rage, knew that he had been visited by a budding sorceress. He was bewildered, but submitted to enchantment. She had thawed him, healed him, had relit the great lamp of his spirit. He felt suddenly that in his new health he was breathing up all the air in the cave; he wanted to knock a hole in the rock wall to let more air in for her. He had to move. He whirled and stamped. She spun with him, screeching with laughter. Her hair whipped about her face.

"What am I doing?" he said.

"Dancing. I am, too."

"Why?"

"Why not?"

"Are we happy or something?"

"I'm very happy here with you, Father. And you're almost happy."

"Why only almost?"

"You won't be completely happy until you're driving the sun chariot again."

Helios stopped dancing in midstride. He stood there, thinking. "I'm thinking," he thought. "I like to think sometimes, but it's hard to start." He couldn't think without using his hands. Thoughtfully, he picked up two boulders and smashed them together. He scattered handfuls of rock dust.

"Stop it!" she cried. "You're making me sneeze."

"You know what I think?" he asked.

"No, what?"

"You said that about me driving the chariot again just because you want a ride."

"Of course I do, if it's you driving. I mean it's not just for the ride, it would have to be you at the reins. I wouldn't want to ride with Apollo, for instance."

"Apollo—pah!" He spat.

"Do you hate him, Father?"

"Of course."

"Suppose, just suppose, you did want to take me for a ride. How would you get the chariot? Steal it?"

"It was stolen from me. It was mine. I'd repossess it."

"How? Can I help? Please let me."

"You'll wait here until I come back for you. That stable is closely guarded. Hundred-handed giants ring it about. It's no place for a little girl."

He did not realize how she had maneuvered him into making her intention his.

"How would you get in past those horrid giants?" she asked. "Won't it be very dangerous?"

"I won't try to get in," he said. "The chariot will come out. I'll stand off and whistle. The stallions will awake and gallop out, dragging the chariot behind them. They love me, those sun horses. It was I who greeted them when they were foaled by the Great Mare. I trained them myself. They obey Apollo now because Zeus has made him their master, but it's me they love. And they'll come when I call."

"And you'll pick me up here? Promise?"

"Not here," said Helios. "The chariot must not swing too low or trees will burn like torches, and the earth scorch. When I leave, you must leave also and climb to the top of our highest mountain, which is Pelion. Go to the very top, stand there at dawn, and I'll scoop you up."

"Oh, Father, I love you so much."

He just grunted, but he was very pleased.

4

The Stolen Sun

he sun chariot was trundling across the sky.
The huge wheels were turning, casting light,
warming and brightening the earth, chasing
the shadows of night. Hot with pride, Helios
was driving. And the great golden stallions, feeling their old
master's hand on the reins, were trumpeting their pleasure as they
went.

Circe stood raptly in the chariot, stretching on tiptoe so
that she might see over the scalloped side at what was passing
below. She saw specks of houses, little humps that were moun-
tains, and splinters that were trees—and, farther off, a purple
smudge of sea.

"Mother is somewhere among those oaks down there," she
thought. "And all the other dryads I know. But even if they're
looking up at the sky they won't see me because we're too high.
Wouldn't they be surprised to know that I'm up here, though
. . . I wonder if they'll believe me when I tell them."

They were passing over tiny cliffs that dropped off into the
puddle of sea. She gasped in pleasure as she saw the water start
to sparkle in the early light. "Lower!" she cried. "Lower, Father!
Go down!"

"Why?"

"I want to see if we can make the water boil."

Helios twitched the reins, putting the horses into a dive. The chariot swooped low over the sea. Circe saw the water bubble and hiss. Steam arose, and a strong, hot chowdery smell as the fish began to cook.

"Phew!" growled Helios. "What a stink!" He shouted to the horses, and they began to climb so steeply that the girl felt herself sliding toward the back of the chariot and clung to her father's waist. She saw gulls, maddened by the smell of boiling fish, diving toward the sea, screaming greedily as they went. She

Helios twitched the reins, and
he and Circe began to climb.

saw them pull up short. The sea was too hot, the steam too thick; they could not alight. And bears and wolves thronged the headland, coming down to the shore to feed, but they, too, were driven back by the heat of the boiling sea.

Screaming with excitement, Circe clung to her father as the chariot careened over the billowing steam. And her screeching was a wild song to Helios, who had never loved anyone before and didn't understand his new, strange feelings. All he knew now was that he would do anything, anything at all, to keep this daughter shrieking so joyously.

"Faster!" he called to his horses. "Go, my golden ones— faster still!"

The great stallions broke into a gallop. The chariot smashed across the sky fifty times faster than it had ever gone before. And folk on earth saw a sight most strange: night pursuing day like a black hound chasing a golden stag. And no sooner had the sky turned black than silver light began to nibble at its eastern rim. Silver turned to pink, to red, to orange. Bars of orange fire branded the horizon, flushing to hot gold, becoming a golden flood of light that washed away the last darkness.

To the gods atop Olympus watching the sun chariot streak by, it seemed that earth's day was flashing on and off like a child playing with a lamp.

"What's happening?" said Zeus to Hera. "Has Apollo gone mad?"

"Ask him," said Hera. "There's your golden boy now racing up the mountain as fast as he can."

"Apollo!" cried Zeus. "Why are you down here with your sun high in the sky?"

"Oh, Father, 'tis not I in the sky. I'm right here, as you can see. Someone has stolen my chariot. And the damned fool is racing the horses without mercy. They'll pull up lame."

"You've lost your chariot? How careless!"

"I didn't lose it. It was stolen, I told you."

Helios fell like a star.

"You allowed yourself to be robbed? By whom?"

"By Helios."

"Him? Are you sure?"

"Very sure. It must be Helios. The horses will allow no one else to drive them. Except me, of course."

"Helios driving the sun chariot?" growled Zeus. "Against my strict edict. He's either very crazy or very brave."

"Probably both," said Hera.

Poseidon suddenly appeared on the mountaintop. The sea god was looking very unlike his elegant self. His hair was matted with boiled seaweed, and a huge, half-cooked stone crab was clinging to his beard. He walked toward Zeus, bellowing: "Do something about Apollo; he's gone mad! The sun is out of control. My sea has turned to steam, and my fish are all cooking."

"I'm here, Uncle!" cried Apollo. "Can't you see? I never touched the reins this morning. Helios stole my chariot. It's he who's driving it so fast, day chasing night, and night chasing day. Oh, Father Zeus, can't you do something?"

"Yes, Brother," said Poseidon. "Do something."

"Yes, Husband! Something . . . anything," said Hera.

He drew back his arm and hurled his thunderbolt. The fiery spear sizzled across the sky and hit Helios in the chest, knocking him out of the chariot. He fell to earth as the masterless horses galloped over the horizon, dragging darkness in their wake—so that Helios, ablaze, fell like a star.

Without hesitation, Circe leaped out after him. Her hair floated, casting a nimbus of light. The steam was still coming off the sea where she fell, slowing her descent. It was like falling into a cloud, falling in a dream. And when she landed it was upon a seabed left by the evaporated tide. She found herself among the corpses of octopi and whales and the skeletons of foundered ships, and she didn't know whether she was awake or asleep; whether a happy dream of her father had turned into nightmare, or whether she had really found her father, and had fallen into this slimy nightmare and would soon awake. But awake or asleep, she had to find him. She moved off along the seabed, among the dead, huge bodies of whales and sharks and manta rays, and threading through the skeletons of sunken ships, calling, "Father . . . Father . . ."

5

The High Council

elios had vanished after being hit by the thunderbolt. He was not dead, Zeus knew. Titans, being of the god breed, are immortal; they can be made to suffer, but cannot die. And Zeus was determined to make Helios suffer as much as possible. He called a meeting of the High Council to organize the pursuit. They met in the great throne room of the cloud castle atop Olympus.

Zeus, clad in his star-encrusted purple judgment robes, sat on a gold and ivory throne, fingering the volt-blue zigzag shaft of lightning he used as a scepter. He addressed the gods briefly, outlining the task.

"I have a question, Your Majesty," said Poseidon. "Do we really need to mobilize such vast forces against one unruly Titan?"

"Well," said Zeus, "if you think back to our war against Cronos and his Titans, you will remember that Helios was one of our most dangerous foes. His strength has not diminished with age—and he seems to have grown more reckless than ever. He will not, I assure you, be easily subdued."

*"The Furies will report to you
this very night, My Lord," said Hades.*

"In any case," said Poseidon, "we have to catch him before we start subduing him."

"Exactly," said Zeus. "And that is why I shall ask Brother Hades to lend us his Furies. In addition to their other formidable skills, they fly so fast, and their noses are so keen for the hunt, that they'll be able to ransack all the corners of earth and heaven for that cursed rebel. Once we take him we'll make sure he's incapable of any further escape, and his endless punishment will begin."

"The Furies will report to you this very night, My Lord," said Hades.

"Our thanks to you, Brother," said Zeus. "And while they're up here they can attend to some other matters. As I mentioned, some of my mortals are getting out of line and need a bit of professional torment to teach them their place. Yes-s-s, your hags will find themselves fully employed."

6

Dione

earching for her father, Circe was walking through a wood in Arcadia. The trees thinned into a clearing; she crossed it heading toward a stand of oaks. She stopped when she saw a big woman standing there. Too tall for a mortal; she seemed to be a goddess. But Circe couldn't tell what she was because her hair was white and her handsome face looked worn, and no goddess, Circe knew, ever aged past her glorious prime. Whatever she was, though, the girl immediately preferred the look of her to anyone she had ever known, except her mother and father. In fact, her wide gray eyes reminded Circe of her dryad mother. Her voice was curious, too—rich but harsh—as she called to Circe.

"You there, stop lurking. I see you."

"I'm not lurking," said Circe. "If I didn't want you to see me I wouldn't have come this close."

"Come closer."

Circe came right to her and looked up into her face. "My name is Circe," she said.

"I am Dione."

"The oak goddess?" cried Circe.

"Well, I used to be."

"*Used* to be?"

"I'm no longer a goddess, but am still an oak something, I suppose."

"I don't understand."

"Can't blame you," said Dione. "I scarcely understand it myself, but it happened."

"What happened exactly? How could you stop being a goddess once you started?"

"I fell in love, shed my divinity, and became a woman."

"Oh, tell me, tell me!" cried Circe. "Whatever you are, I seem to be growing fond of you quite rapidly. Which is odd because I'm coldhearted."

"Who told you that?"

"My mother—many times. Anyway, we must be related. My mother is a dryad of the Oak Clan. Her name is Arlawanda."

"Arlawanda . . . Circe . . . Yes, they're clan names. I'm probably your great-aunt or something. Do you really want to hear my story?"

"Yes, please!"

Circe sat on a stump and looked up at Dione. She saw that the gray eyes were brimming with tears.

Dione said: "Cronos, who gave his name to time, was master of all its cruel tricks. I went to him and pleaded that my husband, who happened to be human, be granted immortality. Cronos pretended to heed my plea. He said that year by year, bit by bit, I might bestow my own immortality upon my husband. And if I managed it skillfully I'd be able to keep him alive for a thousand years and we'd both die at the same time. I accepted the conditions joyfully, for I had no wish to outlive my dear one. And so the bargain was struck, but I didn't realize what a foul trickster Cronos was. For, while I was able to keep my husband alive by shortening my own life, I could not keep him young. And he aged much faster than I did. Kept withering, shrinking . . . Behold him now!"

"I've just found you, Aunt.
Don't go away.
I can't bear another loss."

She pointed to a tree. At first Circe saw nothing, then when she went closer she saw a tiny man leaning against the trunk. No larger than a three-year-old child, he wore a long, grizzled beard, and his skin was as wrinkled as bark.

"I shall lose him soon," said Dione. "If a hawk doesn't take him, or a fox, he'll simply dwindle away till there's nothing left. But he shan't go alone into Hades, poor little darling. I shall take full advantage of my mortality. I shall slay myself, and our shades will embrace as we journey to the Land Beyond Death."

"I've just found you, Aunt. Don't go away. I can't bear another loss."

"Another? What do you know of loss, my child?"

"Too much. A few months ago I tracked down my father, whom I'd never met, and was just teaching him to love me when he was taken."

"How?"

"Well, we were going for a ride in his sun chariot when Zeus hurled a thunderbolt, hitting him square."

"Your father is Apollo?"

"No!" cried Circe. "Not that thief! My father is the true sun god—Helios. Zeus stripped him of his authority and put Apollo in his place. Took away his chariot and his horses and his proud task, and broke his heart—which I was just mending before he vanished."

"What happened? Did he steal the chariot?"

"Not steal; it was his. He repossessed it. Whistled up the horses, who love him, and they came galloping. He didn't mean to keep the chariot. He knew he couldn't. He just wanted it for long enough to take me for a ride. Then slimy Poseidon made some trouble because we boiled a bit of his sea away, and the tyrant, Zeus, flung his fiery shaft. And my father fell from the chariot. I jumped out after him but couldn't find him anyplace. I've been searching and searching."

"Let's try a finding," said Dione.

"What do you mean?"

"I'll try to locate your father for you. Witch me up a fire on that flat rock."

"How do you know I can do that?"

"You have the look of someone who's been dabbling in magic. It's a family trait. Start me a fire so that a daughter's sharp young love can enter the spell—and I'll do the rest."

Circe pointed her hands at a rock, mumbling as she whirled about three times. Pale flame stood upon the stone. Dione cupped one hand in the other; when she opened them they were full of herbs. She dropped the herbs on the fire. The flame leaped. It danced on the rock, spitting purple and green gouts of smoke. Aromatic smoke, very sweet.

Breathing it, Circe felt herself go blank. She didn't know her own name. She was being translated into a place beyond words. In the burning crystal of her new state she saw patches of hard whiteness that might have been snow-covered rock, but were only glimmers of whiteness behind struggling shapes of darkness. She screamed. Nameless horror filled her. Blackness swarmed. Deeper and deeper she sank.

When she awoke it was into fragrant warmth. She found herself in Dione's lap. The great arms cradled her, rocked her gently. She heard her voice coming out in a thready whisper.

"Oh, Dione, I saw things. Horrid, huge, ragged things. Their blackness covered everything. I couldn't see past them."

"Yes," said Dione. "I saw them, too."

"What are they?"

"The Furies."

"Furies?"

"Flying hags. Hell hags. They serve Hades. They hunt down runaway shades and flay them with their stingray whips."

"What are they doing up here?"

"Pursuing your father."

"Why would Hades send them? It was only Zeus my father offended. Well, and Poseidon and Apollo, too, perhaps. But not Hades."

"Ah, my child," said Dione, "while the gods quarrel among themselves, they tend to help each other when there's an important cruelty to be done."

"But I didn't see my father. Just those things flying."

"It means they're pursuing him hotly, but haven't caught him yet. Helios is very powerful and resourceful. It may be that they'll never catch him. But they'll keep trying, you can be sure of that."

"Then I must leave immediately," declared Circe. "I must find him before they do."

"Then what?"

"Help him fight the Furies, of course."

"You're a very brave girl, but you're not ready to fight the Furies, not even one of them, let alone three. As you are now, you wouldn't last the wink of an eye. You must prepare yourself before you go against them."

"How?"

"You must grow into your full strength. And while you're doing so, you must learn real sorcery. I will teach you."

Circe felt a sharp pain in her calf. She kicked out, heard a squealing, and saw Dione's little man sprawled on the ground. She was amazed when Dione slapped her, and tumbled her off her lap.

"You kicked him, you wicked girl," shouted Dione.

She scooped up her husband and held him to her, kissing him.

"Something was pinching my leg," said Circe. "I didn't know it was him. I just kicked. Why was he pinching me?"

Circe kicked out, heard a squealing,
and saw Dione's little man sprawled on the ground.

"He was jealous because you were sitting in my lap. That's his place, he thinks; no one else belongs there."

Circe saw that the little man, high above her, safe in his wife's arms, was grinning down at her. "He's rather childish for his age, isn't he," she said.

"He is, he is," said Dione mournfully. "Everything about him has shrunk—his mind and his spirit, too. But I love him just the same, even more, perhaps. And if you're going to stay here with me, you must learn to love him, too, and not hurt him in any way."

"I'll try," muttered Circe.

"You must do more than try," said Dione. "You must succeed."

Circe looked up at the husband again. His eyes twinkled pure malice; he stuck his tongue out.

"All right," she said. "But do you think you could tell him not to pinch me?"

"Have you ever had a puppy or a kitten?" asked Dione.

"Oh, yes, lots of them. They're dogs and cats now, and waiting for me at my mother's place. I miss them."

"Well," said Dione, "you didn't mind when a kitten scratched you or a puppy nipped you, did you? You didn't kick them, I'm sure. Can't you look at him the same way?"

"Yes, I really will try," said Circe.

She knew there was something wrong with Dione's comparison; nevertheless, she was determined to learn sorcery, and knew that to do that she would have to put up with the little man, or at least pretend to.

7

Sorcery Lessons

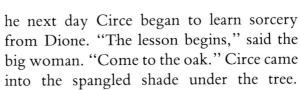he next day Circe began to learn sorcery from Dione. "The lesson begins," said the big woman. "Come to the oak." Circe came into the spangled shade under the tree. "Now, cast off your garment," said Dione, "and I shall do likewise. For you must enter sorcery with your whole body. You must feel the wind on you, birdcall must enter you, and you must know the touch of this mighty oak—the living totem of our clan whose taproot drinks the blood of mutilated gods."

Circe shed her tunic. She felt sequins of hot sunlight upon her, felt the fingers of the wind searching her. A musk of summer grass beat about her, threaded with birdcall. Screaming with joy, lithe as a cat, she sprang to a lower limb of the tree. Dione doffed her tunic. Unclothed, she seemed larger. She easily lifted herself into the tree.

But then the little husband dashed out from behind the trunk and began to jump up and down, blubbering and bawling. "Oh, dear," murmured Dione. She swung down, lifted him in one hand and climbed up again. She stood him on her knee and passed her hand over his face, whispering, "Sleep, sleep . . . Do not weep, my dearie, but sleep, sleep . . ."

He slumped on her lap, fast asleep. "Come up here," she said to Circe. The girl climbed to the upper limb and sat beside her. And, to her dismay, was handed the sleeping husband. "Here," said Dione.

"What shall I do with him?"

"Please don't use that tone. He's not really a slug or a snail, you know. Just hold him carefully and roll him up in my hair so that he rests against my back between my shoulders. He'll sleep soundly there, and I'll be able to start our lesson without interruption."

Circe took the little man, holding him gently, although she yearned to twist his ears. She wrapped him in Dione's thick, fragrant hair and rolled him up until he hung against her back between her shoulder blades, snoring slightly.

"Thank you," said Dione. "Now swing down to your own branch and make yourself comfortable. We have a lot to cover."

To do magic," said Dione, "is to tamper with nature, and the risk is enormous. For a spell gone wrong will not only destroy its target; it will turn and rend whoever has wrought the spell."

"Worth the risk, it seems to me," said Circe.

"Does it? Well, hearken now. There are two kinds of magic."

"Good and bad?"

"Yes."

"But so is everything else—either good or bad," said Circe.

"Magic even more so," said Dione. "It's always more so, in every way. Witchcraft is evil magic, cruelly twisting nature and wrenching things out of their form and their own meaning, and changing them into something worse, always worse. Sorcery is good magic. It looks into the essence of living forms, and when it *trans*forms something it is always within the nature of what it really is, only more so."

"I'm not sure I understand," said Circe.

"I'll give you an example," said Dione. "Ages ago, when I was young and this oak was just a sapling, there was a young hunter who roamed the forest. He was a pretty lad, very brave and merry, and I grew fond of him. I did not make myself known to him, but watched him, kept watching, for I enjoyed the sight of him. And I noted that toward the close of day he lost his

*"To do magic is to tamper with nature,
and the risk is enormous."*

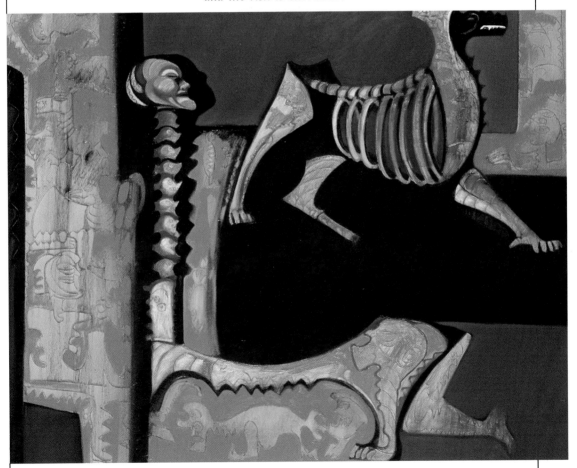

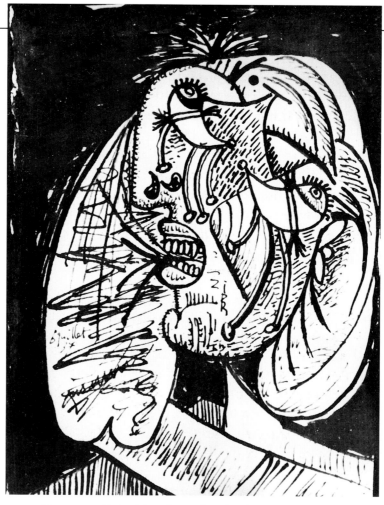

She was a little thing for such a loud voice.
Not bad looking if her face hadn't been twisted
by all the rage that was in her.

merriment, grew sad, in fact. And when he left the wood and
turned toward what I thought must be his home, his sprightly
gait changed, his footsteps dragged.

"So I followed him home one dusk and learned the reason.
Followed him to a trim little cottage which he must have built
with his own hands, and saw him enter. And heard a voice start
up. A woman's voice, a young one, but with no sweetness. Harsh,
rasping, mean, accusatory. Occasionally, he spoke a soft answer,
which made her screech. I peered in and saw her. She was a little

thing for such a loud voice. Not bad looking if her face hadn't been twisted by all the rage that was in her.

"Well, I felt that I had to do something, and did it that very night. He awoke to find her gone. He mourned for a few days, but I taught him to forget his loss and count his blessings."

"What did you do to the woman?" asked Circe. "Kill her?"

"Oh, no, no, no. I worked a good magic. Abrupt but good. I turned her into a jaybird. She flew off, found herself a blue-crested mate and happily scolded him all day long. And is not angered by soft replies, for he scolds also."

"And you call that a good magic?"

"Certainly. You see, she was really meant to be a jay from the first, or a raving bitch, perhaps, but something went askew. In her soul's journey toward birth she took a wrong turn some-where. And was full of mysterious rage and unhappiness until I turned her back into what she should have been in the first place."

"Why not a bitch, then, since you didn't like her?"

"Well, I actually do like dogs; they're usually sweeter-tem-pered than birds, even the vicious ones. Besides, she was really more birdlike than doglike. Yes, it was a good magic, Circe. Slightly selfish, but basically good. I made both of them happy; him, perhaps, more. But things can't always be equal."

"Well, I'm glad to hear that was a good magic. It still leaves the sorceress quite free, doesn't it?"

"All you're free to do now, my girl, is learn. And the lessons are quite hard. Every herb that heals or harms. All the spook words of benefit or bane. Charm-rhymes plain and puzzling. And countercharms for everything, of course, so that you may combat witches and evil wizards—and undo your own mistakes."

8

Salmoneus

Salmoneus, king of Aeolis, was very rich and powerful, but he was gnawed by dissatisfaction. "King . . . king . . . ," he muttered to himself. "It's better to be one than not, but it's still not much. Every piddling little state has someone who wears a crown and squats on a throne and calls himself king, so the title is not sufficiently revered. Take me, for example, ruler of a big, warlike country which is getting bigger all the time as it gobbles up its neighbors—even I, who am outgrowing kingship and becoming an emperor, am not paid enough honor. Oh, I'm feared and obeyed, but I'm not *worshiped*. People are afraid of me because they know that extremely unpleasant things will happen to them if they don't exhibit wholesome terror—which is all very well— but the idea of me doesn't awe them, overwhelm them, cause them to fall on their silly faces and worship. And that's because I'm still only a man and not a god. I can't stand it any longer. I must find a way to be more than I am. But how? There's a way . . . there must be a way."

He thought and thought and finally decided what to do. He sent heralds throughout the land, to every city and town and

This day was called the Day of Justice.

village. They announced that Zeus, ruler of heaven, had honored the nation by choosing its own king to represent god power here below; not merely as priests do, but as the very embodiment, on certain occasions, of the divine will on earth.

Whereupon Salmoneus ordered an enormous marble pedestal to be built in the courtyard in front of the palace. Upon this pedestal a golden throne was set, even larger and more splendid than the one inside the palace, and studded with diamonds and rubies and sapphires. Above the throne was spread a canopy of gold-threaded silk and peacock feathers to shade him from the sun.

And to the great square in front of the palace in the capital city of Elis were summoned the populace. One day each month everyone was required to attend. This day was called the Day of Justice. Anyone who felt himself wronged in life in any way could appeal to the king. And he, with the wisdom and power conferred upon him by almighty Zeus, would render judgment, declaring either that the unlucky one deserved his bad luck, or that he had been unjustly used by fate and was due for a change in fortune.

Of course, Salmoneus cared nothing about the pleas themselves. He would listen with less than half an ear, and his decision would be based on whether the plaintiff happened to please or displease him. Nor were bribes discouraged. Often, Salmoneus made no decision at all, but postponed the matter, because he enjoyed the feeling of keeping people in suspense.

But the real point of this entire business was the closing ceremony, which was held at dusk. Then Salmoneus would arise from his throne, stand tall upon the pedestal, lifting his face to heaven and stretching his arms high, and quiver for a while, uttering low, ecstatic moans, as if the power of Zeus were an actual current flowing down from Olympus and entering him as he stood there.

Then servants would rush to him bearing brass pots, which he would clang together to imitate thunder. Others would come bearing torches, which he would snatch from them and hurl in the air to mimic lightning. And the great crowd had been rehearsed to fall on its knees at this moment, shouting, "Glory, glory, glory to our god, Salmoneus!"

9

Jealousy

For some time now Circe had dwelt in the oak grove, learning the art of sorcery as fast as Dione could teach. And her body grew along with her mind. Her legs grew very long and suavely muscled. Rose over bronze was her skin, and the rich mane of her hair seemed woven of light. All in all, she was a sleek, powerful young nymph, taller now than Dione, bursting with health, and casting a fragrance of sunshine and crushed grass.

Upon this day Circe and Dione were lying on a flat rock near the river's edge, letting the sun dry them after their swim. Circe was amused, for Dione had caught her husband and bathed him—something he hated. She had disregarded his complaints, and scrubbed and dried and oiled him rather roughly. And he had rushed off, cursing.

"You know," said Circe, "he seems to have stopped shrinking."

"I've noticed," said Dione.

Circe was puzzled by her tone. "What's wrong?" she asked.

"Nothing."

"Yes there is."

"Well," said Dione. "He's not only stopped shrinking, he's

stopped glaring at you and doing little mischiefs. Or haven't you noticed?"

"I have, and I'm glad, of course."

"Don't you know what that means?"

"What?"

"The little fool is falling under your spell. Not one I've taught you. Nobody had to teach you. You cast this spell as naturally as a rose putting out her scent to pull a bee into her cup. Yes, yes, I know it's not your fault. You can't help being so young and beautiful, damn you."

"Do you want me to go away?"

"We are going away, you and I, for a little while. To Elis to attend Judgment Day."

"What's that?"

"King Salmoneus claims that once every month he is invested with the authority of Zeus and can change the fortune of anyone who had been treated unjustly by the gods."

"Do you believe that?"

"I don't believe or disbelieve," said Dione. "I'm willing to be shown. I shall appeal to him to undo the treachery of Cronos and grant me another thousand years with my husband. I shall also pray that the poor tyke be released from the spell you have cast. No, no, don't say it. I know what I know."

"I'm sorry, Dione."

"And while we're there you can ask the king to aid you in finding your father. I don't know whether he'll want to since it is Zeus your father offended. Isn't that your story?"

"It's what happened. In any case, I shan't be coming back here. How can I live with you if you feel this way?"

"Yes, perhaps it would be better for you to resume your journey. There's not much more I can teach you, anyway."

Aeolis lay on the other side of the mountain; the road there lay through valley and wood. But Circe and Dione walked tirelessly with an easy, swinging gait. They didn't speak much on the way; each was wrapped in her own thoughts. Of course, what Circe was thinking about was what Dione had said.

"He's such a treacherous little thing," she said to herself. "I don't think he hates me a bit less than he ever did. I think this is just a new trick. He's pretending to fall in love with me just to make Dione jealous. Yes, of course, that must be it. He's found the one sure way to turn her against me. Oh, if it were only possible to give him what he deserves. How I would enjoy getting my hands on him. Pooh! What's the difference? I'll never see him again. This chapter of my life is ending, and I'm ready for a new one to begin."

10

Judgment Day

s they neared the city they passed other people going there, and everyone seemed to be staring at them. Dione drew Circe into a fringe of trees at the side of the road.

"It's no good," she said. "You're attracting too much attention."

"Me? They're staring at both of us."

"It's you they're looking at, and no wonder. You're much too beautiful to go unnoticed."

She reached up and pulled two leaves from a branch. She held them above her head, mumbling. The leaves turned to two long brown cloaks, with cowls attached.

"Here," she said. "Put it on."

"It's so ugly," said Circe.

"That's the idea. Get it on and stoop and huddle as you walk so that you won't look so tall. And be sure to cover your hair with that cowl."

"But why? I don't mind them looking at me. I rather enjoy it. I've never been in a city before."

"Do as I say," gritted Dione. "Put it on immediately, or you'll spoil everything."

"How?"

"If you stand in that crowd towering above everyone, flashing your bare arms and legs and that mass of hair, why, they'll all be gawking at you. And the king will see them doing it, and grow furious. He doesn't like anyone to notice anyone else when he's there—especially on his day of divinity. And if he falls into a fit of temper, instead of doing us any favors he'll be more likely to do some very unpleasant things. So please put the cloak on without any more argument."

Circe snatched the cloak and flung it over her, covering her hair with the cowl, but she was fuming inside. "I'll get rid of it as soon as possible," she said to herself. "When the king summons her to the throne she'll be too busy to notice me at all, and I'll do as I like. I can't believe the change in her, and all because of that little toad of a husband."

But as she humped along in her cloak, she saw that Dione's tactic was working. No one stared at them. They entered the city and made their way through thronged streets to the courtyard, which was mobbed. Dione, using her strength, elbowed her way to the front of the crowd and stood near the pedestal—and Circe followed.

The king sat on his throne. His robe was purple, encrusted with silver stars. His scepter was blue and of a zigzag shape to imitate the scepter of Zeus, which was a lightning bolt. Gilded boots he wore, with very high heels, and a tall, spiked, golden crown sat on his head. Circe couldn't see much face because he wore an enormous fleecy white beard à la Zeus, obviously false.

"But he'd look worse without it," thought Circe. "How can anyone believe that he's a god?"

A young herald stood near the throne, holding a scroll. At a signal from the king, he read out a name. A man emerged from the crowd and climbed marble stairs to the pedestal, then knelt before the throne. He mumbled to the king, too low for Circe to hear. The king interrupted him with a wave of his hand. The man pulled himself to his feet and left. He was slinking away, Circe noticed, as if whatever he had asked had been denied.

Dione stood erect beside her, motionless, staring at the king. "Does she still really believe in this nonsense?" thought Circe. "Can't she see he's a fake?" Then, as the herald began to read out another name, she felt a kind of shiver pass through the closely packed crowd, like a wind passing through a wheat field.

She looked up and saw why.

At that time, when the world was new, there were no bats. The only mammal that flew was the lupalia, which in Greek means "winged wolf." Indeed, the body slung between the wings was as big as a wolf's, its jaws even more powerful, its wingspread greater than an eagle's. It ate only meat—live meat—which meant deer, mountain goats, sheep, cows, and the occasional brave shepherd who tried to protect his herd. The only good thing about the lupalia was that it disliked towns and villages and loathed cities, and folk who did not roam the wild places were fairly safe from this savage beast.

Upon this day, therefore, when the crowd gathered before the palace of Salmoneus saw three enormous creatures flying overhead, its first terrified thought was, "three lupalia . . . what are they doing over a city?"

The creatures were coming lower, in slow swoops, and people were beginning to scream and panic. But were they lupalia? Their wings were glinting strangely; their claws glittered. And by the time the horrified Elians realized that what they were seeing were not flying wolves but flying hags with brass wings and claws, the Furies were in a steep dive toward the golden throne.

Salmoneus, watching them, was petrified; he could not move.

What the Elians saw then they were never to forget. The sight branded itself on their memory and deviled their sleep. Night after night, for years afterward, they awoke whimpering.

And the tale of that day when the Furies came was used to frighten children into pious behavior for generations to come.

Alecto and Megaera unslung their whips as they dived. The king awoke from his stupor and tried to scramble away, but they caught him. Hovering low, they snapped their whips. The lashes whistled through the air toward the king, not flogging him but binding him. One lash curled about his neck, the other about his ankles. The hags pulled on their whips, stretching him horizontally just over the pediment, then, still hovering, moving in perfect, horrid rhythm, they flailed him up and down, smashing his body against the marble.

The Royal Guard had been stationed in back of the throne, but not one guardsman defended his king; they were paralyzed by fear. When they were able to move, it was backward, off the pediment, to vanish in the crowd.

Circe felt Dione trembling beside her. She could tell that Dione was not afraid. Her face was flushed bright red with rage. She uttered a wordless roar. Circe grasped her arm, trying to hold her back, but Dione shook off her hand and rushed forward. She leaped onto the pediment, caught one lash, and tried to break it. The hags screeched and dropped their whips.

The king lay on the marble, and Dione saw that she couldn't have helped him. The man who had played god had been pounded to a pulp–split open like a rotten melon. Now the Furies, all three of them, seized Dione and flew up with her. Circling slowly above the crowd, they struck at her with their claws, raking her to shreds with their brass talons. Leisurely, they tore her to pieces. Bloody gobbets of her who had been Circe's teacher dropped from the Furies' claws, but never hit the ground because they were caught by screaming gulls.

Circe slipped through the crowd. She flung off her cloak and raced away like a deer. There was something she had to do. Her tall legs flashed, her bright hair flew, and people thought it was the goddess Artemis, hunting a stag.

The creatures were coming lower, in slow swoops.
The king awoke from his stupor and tried to scramble away.

She didn't stop until she had reached the oak grove, and
didn't rest then. Dione had built her husband a little stone house
so that he might shelter safely at the rare times she left the grove.
Circe ran to that house, reached into the door, and plucked the
little man out. She lifted him, holding him before her face and
studying him as if she had never seen him before.

The red light of failing day sifted through the oak leaves,
setting them ablaze. An owl who awaited darkness hooted
hungrily.

"Where's Dione?" quavered the little man.

"Dead."

"Oh, my. Who'll look after me?"

"Is that all you have to say?"

"You'll have to take care of me now."

"I'll take care of you, all right."

"Why do you say it like that?" he whined. "Why are you looking at me that way? You're frightening me."

"Am I, now?"

"Be nice. Please."

"I'm going to be nice. I'm about to do Dione, whom you turned against me, a final favor. I'm sending you to keep her company."

"Don't kill me. I don't want to die."

"Don't you? But she gave up her immortality so that she might not outlive you. What an ungrateful little rat you are. Rat. Yes."

She shifted her grip so that he dangled upside down. Slowly turning, she crooned:

Meager, selfish,
ceaselessly mean.
Scurviest rascal
ever seen.
Form must follow content,
and you shall be
what you were meant
to be.
I'll see to that!
Drop your human guise,
Reduce your puny size,
Return to RAT!

She felt the leg she was holding change in her hand; it became thin, whiplike. She looked down and saw that she held a rat by the tail. It arched up and glared at her out of poisonous little red eyes. It curled up farther and tried to bite her hand. She snapped her wrist and it fell back.

She glanced at the sun. Only a red tab was left and that was going; shadows flowed after it. Circe hooted like an owl.

With no rustle of leaves an owl appeared on a lower branch;
its huge circular eyes caught what light was left.

With no rustle of leaves an owl appeared on a lower branch; its huge circular eyes caught what light was left. Circe swung the rat around and around by the tail, then slung it into the air. She had aimed it well. The owl caught it without leaving its bough. Clutched it in her claws just as the Furies had clutched Dione, and flew away.

"He's lucky," thought Circe. "Owls kill quickly. A few seconds of pain and his shade will join Dione's. Why she should want that shabby little soul with her throughout eternity is something I'll never understand. Love is a mystery. I wonder if I'll ever love anyone that much. I guess I'm too coldhearted. Oh, well . . ."

11

Athena

Quarrels flared frequently in the Pantheon and grew into feuds. But since gods live forever, and forever takes so long, they learned that keeping the same enemy grows boring after a while, so the feuds healed themselves.

There was one high feud, however, that was never healed, but went on and on, growing worse every century. For Athena, Goddess of Wisdom, hated her uncle Poseidon so fiercely that she could never make peace with him, and he returned her hatred full force. Although the Maid in Armor could not match the sea god physically—she did not own his mastery of wind and tide— she could outthink him, and was always weaving plots.

Now, the owl was Athena's favorite bird and she had given it the gift of wisdom. She had chosen a great gray owl as her special adviser. He flew here and there, spying for her, picking up snippets of information, doing various confidential errands— and, between missions, perched on her shoulder.

Birds are great gossips, even owls who look so solemn and

judgelike. And what happens to one soon becomes known to all. Thus, when Athena's owl heard from an Arcadian bird how a young oak nymph named Circe had changed a little man into a rat and was thoughtful enough to feed it to the owl, the goddess heard the tale soon after.

Now, Athena had been very busy the last year or so, launching a new attack on Poseidon. What she had done was plant various hazards about the islands of the Middle Sea so that ships would disappear, crews would vanish, and seamen everywhere, who had been Poseidon's most ardent worshipers, would lose faith in him and turn to other gods. And nothing wounds a god more than losing worshipers. For only when he is praised and feared and adored does a god feel fully alive.

Athena had planted many a hidden reef that could tear the bottom out of a ship. Jagged rocks and whirlpools she dropped into the Middle Sea, and various monsters—the man-eating Cyclopes she had led to one island, and settled the iron-headed Amycus, who butted people to death, on another isle. Winged naiads called Sirens she had stationed on certain rocks. In their voices dwelt the chuckle of tide over pebbles and the lisp of rain, birdcall and wind sigh. And when they perched on the rocks, singing, their song scattered the wits of helmsmen who steered their ships onto the rocks.

Athena observed with glee the rising toll of lost ships and lost sailors, and the way Poseidon's altars were drawing fewer worshipers with each shipwreck. She exulted in the sea god's mounting wrath. But for all her success she was not satisfied. And when she was told of the lovely young sorceress who could change a man into a rat and coolly feed him to an owl, she became very interested.

"Thank you," she said to the big gray bird. "This is a juicy bit of information. I can use a girl with that kind of talent."

She stood on the peak of Olympus, breathing in the mingled fragrance of a west wind and thinking hard, trying to recall all

She had stationed winged naiads
called Sirens on certain rocks.

she could about Circe and Helios, and the stolen sun chariot and forbidden ride.

"Yes," she said to herself. "She must still bear a grudge, which would make her want to go along with what I have in mind."

Whereupon she flew off to find Circe.

"Hey, you," he growled to Circe.

Knowing that Circe was half dryad of the Oak Clan, she searched among stands of oak, and found her in a grove in Argos, sitting on a fallen log, combing her hair with a silver comb. Athena heard someone coming through the trees and made herself invisible.

Shambling out of the woods came a huge, hairy man carrying a club. "Hey, you," he growled to Circe.

"Good morning," she said calmly.

"I've come to get you," he said.

"Really? Then what?"

"Take you back to our cave."

"How many of you are there?" asked Circe.

"Twelve, fifteen. Depends how many are left alive at the end of the day."

"And what would I do in your cave?"

"Place is a mess. Big healthy wench like you could do a lot of cooking and cleaning for us. And see to . . . other comforts."

"Interesting," she murmured. "Suppose I were to tell you I didn't want to do that?"

"Look. If you don't come along nicely, I'll just hit you over the head and carry you there."

Circe arose from the log, stood to her full height, raised her arms, and slowly began to twirl, crooning:

Not there
nor anywhere
for you are now
a BEAR.

Indeed, instead of the bearded bandit, a big black bear now stood in the grove. He dropped to all fours and came toward Circe, growling. She snapped her fingers. He stood on his hind legs and began to dance. He danced up to her. She put her hand on his shoulder and danced a few steps with him, then patted his head and shoved him away. He dropped to all fours and shambled back into the forest.

Athena made herself visible and stepped into the clearing. Circe saw a very tall, stern-looking maiden, wearing helmet and breastplate, bearing spear and shield. "You are Athena," she said.

"And you are Circe. I am pleased that you recognize me, though we've never met."

"My father, Helios, described you all to me." She smiled. "And your appearance is quite distinctive, you know."

"So is yours, my dear, so is yours. It is your father I've come to speak to you about, among other things."

"He didn't have much good to say about your family," said Circe. "They treated him cruelly."

"Not me," said Athena. "I didn't have anything to do with all that. I always admired him, as a matter of fact."

"Well, no, he didn't have anything really bad to say about you. Or Hermes."

"You know," said Athena, "our family is not a single loving unit. We all certainly do not hold the same opinion about things, and can quarrel very fiercely among ourselves. For example, I loathe my father's brother, Poseidon. For years we've been feuding with each other."

"Poseidon," murmured Circe. "Tell me more."

Athena then told her how she had been attacking the sea god, trying to rob him of worshipers. How she had dropped rocks and reefs and whirlpools into the Middle Sea to wreck shipping. And how, on various islands, she had planted monsters as a menace to navigation. "But," she said, "all this is not sufficient. Word gets about very quickly among seamen, and they are learning to avoid these perils. I need someone like you to dwell upon an island and provide such enchantments as will draw fleets and their crews to that place, where you will make sure they stay. Will you do it? Will you serve me? The rewards will be great."

He dropped to all fours
and shambled back into the forest.

"I'd like to help you," said Circe. "I, too, hate Poseidon. It was he who complained to Zeus about my father, just because we rode low and cooked a few fish. I'd enjoy doing mischief to his mildewed majesty."

"Then it's settled!" cried Athena. "Splendid!"

"Not quite settled," said Circe. "I can't take on any duties yet. I must search for my father. I've vowed to find him if he's still alive, and I don't even know if he is."

"Perhaps I can help you there," said Athena.

"How?"

"Hearken. Helios is not the only Titan who has been made to disappear but not to die. Uranus, the First One, was beheaded by his son, Cronos, who then cut him to pieces and buried him in a thousand different places. And each one of these thousand graves swarms with life. From the vital mud of the god's decay sprang a rich grass whose seeds fed worms into giant size. And these worms put on leather hide, sprouted wings and spiked tails, and became dragons. From other sites of the First One's burial grew fruit trees of magical nourishment. Then Cronos himself was deposed by Zeus and no one knows what happened to him. Some say that he, like his father, was chopped up and the pieces scattered. Others say that he escaped intact, hid somewhere, and is gathering forces to counterattack. None of us really knows, but my guess is that he's very much alive and still as dangerous as his name, which means time. The point of all this is that I'm sure that your father, who was once so hotly alive, is still smouldering somewhere. Perhaps not in his own form, but still Helios, still casting unique heat. Well, these are deep mysteries, perilous questions. The heirs of murdered kings don't like those who meddle in their secrets. But someone somewhere must have a clue about the whereabouts of Helios. None go to as many places as seamen. And if you catch sailors and take them to your island you will be able to learn all they know before you do other things to them. And I shall help you. I'll make it a point to learn what I can and tell you what I know."

"Will you help me against the Furies?"

"If they threaten you, yes."

"Suppose I want to threaten them?"

"You are a cool one. Well, we'll see. Now go to your isle,

which lies off the huge island of Trinacia. The name of yours is the sound the wind makes—*Aiee*. It's a beautiful place, hilly, rich in oaks, abounding in herbs. You will be able to practice a special sorcery there."

"Let our pact be made, O Goddess," said Circe, bowing before Athena.

"Arise, young friend. The pact shall be observed. And we shall both prosper."

She vanished. And Circe laughed with pleasure.

12

Final Enchantments

For many centuries, then, Circe dwelt on the island of Aiee and served Athena well. She taught herself a spell that allowed her to shift the winds about her island, blowing Trinacia-bound ships into her harbor. Hungry crews disembarked and were drawn by the savors of roasting meat to her courtyard. There a spitted ox was turning over a fire, crackling, sending out a smell that made the sailors slaver with greed.

A beautiful, golden-haired woman then appeared and invited them all into dinner—where they glutted themselves and drank heavily of spiced wine. They fell asleep at the table; when they awoke, they were animals. She had read their natures and turned them into the various beasts they resembled: lion, bear, wolf. Pig, weasel, monkey. Some into birds and fish.

Among the ships that came was that of the great war chief, Ulysses, who had fought in Troy for ten years and had been wandering the sea for ten more, trying to get home but meeting disaster after disaster. This crew, half-starving, had rushed to Circe's castle while their captain followed more slowly.

Circe watched the men gorging themselves and turned them all to swine. When Ulysses came charging into the castle demanding that his men be restored to him, she was about to turn him into a fox. But she changed her mind. His fiery red-gold hair reminded her of Helios; his knotted bronzed arms gave off a musky heat like a ripe field awaiting the last harvest of the year. For the first time since she had lost her father she felt her cold heart thawing.

She undid her magic, restored his men to their own shapes, and begged him to stay with her. He agreed. Her beauty enchanted him. They had fallen under each other's spell, but she was the one most transformed—into a loving warm woman.

Although she offered to share her immortality with him, she could not keep him. For after ten years of war and ten years of wandering, he loved his wife Penelope more than ever, and knew he had to return to her.

So he sailed away and never came back. But they never forgot each other.

Athena, always vigilant, soon learned what had happened and feared that a brokenhearted Circe might lose her magical powers. She decided, therefore, to bring her some information she had been saving for an emergency. The goddess visited the island of Aiee and appeared before Circe, who sat on a rock looking out to sea, toward where she had seen Ulysses' sail disappear.

"Greetings," said Athena. "I bring you good news."

"Thank you, Goddess, but there is only one piece of news that I would consider good, and that I shall never hear. For he has vowed never to return, and he keeps his vows."

"Try this," said Athena. "I know where your father can be found."

Circe sprang to her feet. "Where?" she cried.

"In Tartarus. No, he's not dead. On the contrary, he has chosen a very safe hiding place, for who would think of seeking him there where no one goes voluntarily? But there he dwells in a great roasting pit, disguised as a working fire."

"I want him here—with me! What can I do?"

"Gently, gently. I'm about to tell you what you can do. Although the risk is considerable. You many be torn to pieces doing it."

"Tell me, tell me!"

"Well, you know that the Furies nurse a grudge against you."

"Do they? They haven't bothered me. I haven't seen them since they carried off Dione."

"No, they don't dare attack you while you're up here under my protection. But on their home grounds—that will be quite different."

"Their home grounds? You mean Tartarus?"

"Yes. I know that now I have told you, you will make an attempt to rescue your father. If you rush down there without a plan you will end up in bloody fragments just as Dione did. But I am known as Mistress of Tactics, and will provide you with a plan. A very risky one, but it's your only chance. Now, listen well . . ."

W hen she chose to, Circe could run so lightly over a field that she did not bend the grass. And she drifted lightly now over the hot ashes of Tartarus. She drifted slowly, offering herself as bait to the Furies. She had located the great roasting pit where her father hid but had not revealed herself to him. She was waiting for the Furies to attack.

Now, far off, she heard them screeching. She sprang into the air and floated whitely over the roasting pit, sheathing herself in her own coolness because the heat was terrible.

The screeching grew louder. She saw three black shapes diving at her, wings and claws glinting in the ruddy firelight. She floated there, waiting. Just as they were about to grasp her in their claws, she slipped away like a blown leaf. But they were hurtling so fast they couldn't quite stop their dive. They spread their wings, skidding in the air.

And Helios arose from the pit, and in a wild mimicry of

Circe returned to her island
and continued to weave spells
in the service of Athena.

affection took the hags into his fiery embrace. Black shapes threshed violently. There was a shrieking, a roaring. Flame wrestled with shadows.

The fire was broken, scattered, flared separately here and there. But the Furies had vanished. Scorched rags were all that was left of them. But the hags were immortal; the vital force was still in them. The black, scorched rags fledged into bats, thousands of bats, who immediately flew away to find caves in the upper world.

Helios divided into flame, and lived separate lives. He lives still, some say, as marsh fire, will-o'-the-wisp, wherever wandering fires are seen. Others say something worse: that Helios, vowing to avenge himself upon the world, has squeezed himself into a tiny space without losing his strength. For he knows that man, the questioner, the toolmaker, will one day search out his hiding place, will rudely force it open and release a compressed fire, hot as the sun—scorching earth and sky and all above, below, and between.

Circe, given new hope by the sight of her father and the destruction of the Furies, returned to her island and continued to weave spells in the service of Athena—until the old gods vanished and no one believed in magic anymore.

But Circe, as has been told, was immortal, which means that she is still alive somewhere, although no one knows where. She no longer turns people into beasts. She feels it's unnecessary; they're doing too good a job of it themselves. Besides, she chooses to live quietly and not draw attention to herself. But she is a sorceress still, and keeps in practice. What she does is change an occasional animal into a person.

So if you meet a girl with green eyes and feel you've met her somewhere before and want very much to meet her again, don't fight the feeling. She may have been a cat of yours who wandered away and never came back, one that you've never been able to forget. What you must do is look very carefully at her fingernails. If she can pull them in and stick them out again, then you can be sure that your lost cat is now a found girl.

But be careful. She scratches.

Acknowledgments

Letter Cap Illustrations by Hrana L. Janto

Cover, ERINNYES *(1989) by Hrana L. Janto (12 1/2″ × 14 3/4″)*
  Courtesy of the artist

Opposite page 1, *Detail from* THE BATTLE OF ISSUS *by Albrecht Altdorfer (ca. 1480–1538), oil on wood (62″ × 47″)*
    Courtesy of the Alte Pinakothek, Munich
      Photo: Scala/Art Resource, NY

Page 2, AURORA, *by Guido Reni (1575–1642), ceiling fresco*
    Courtesy of the Casino Rospigliosi, Rome
      Photo: Scala/Art Resource, NY

Page 4, MASK OF COMEDY *(ca. 1st century B.C), detail from a Roman pavement mosaic*
    Courtesy of the Vatican
      Photo: Scala/Art Resource, NY

Page 7, ADORATION OF THE SHEPHERDS *by Jacopo Bassano (ca. 1510–92), oil on canvas*
    Courtesy of the Galleria Borghese, Rome
      Photo: Scala/Art Resource, NY

Page 9, CHARIOT *(ca. 1st century B.C.), Greco-Roman cameo restored by Benvenuto Cellini*
    Courtesy of the Archaeological Museum, Florence
      Photo: Art Resource, NY

Page 10, FALL OF THE REBEL ANGELS *(1986) by Earl Staley, acrylic on canvas (20″ × 16″)*
    Courtesy of the artist and the Ruth Siegel Gallery, NY

Page 13, *Detail from* THE INFERNO *by Nardo di Cione (1343–65), fresco in the Strozzi Chapel, Florence*
      Photo: Scala/Art Resource, NY

Page 14, SATAN *by Jean-Jacques Feuchère (1807–52), bronze enlargement (1850) of the original plaster (h. 31″)*
    Courtesy of the Los Angeles County Museum of Art, Times Mirror Foundation

Page 16, UNTITLED *by Jackson Pollock (1912–56), brush and ink, wax, acrylic on paper (66.0 cm × 52.1 cm)*
 Courtesy of the Metropolitan Museum of Art, gift of Lee Krasner Pollock, 1982 (1982.127.36)

Page 19, GIRL IN MOURNING *by Paul Klee (1879–1940), gouache, pastel, and charcoal on wove paper mounted on light cardboard (23 3/4" × 17 1/2")*
 Courtesy of the Metropolitan Museum of Art, the Berggruen Klee Collection, 1984 (1984.315.61)

Page 22, ECHO (NUMBER 25, 1951) *by Jackson Pollock, enamel on canvas (7' 7 7/8" × 7' 2")*
 Courtesy of the Museum of Modern Art, NY, acquired through the Lillie P. Bliss Bequest and the Mr. and Mrs. David Rockefeller Fund

Page 26, THE CHARIOT OF APOLLO *by Odilon Redon (1840–1916), oil on canvas*
 Courtesy of the Louvre, Paris
  Photo: Giraudon/Art Resource, NY

Page 28, HELIOS RISING FROM THE SEA *(500–490 B.C.), black-figured Greek vase attributed to the Sappho Painter, terra-cotta (h. 7 1/16")*
 Courtesy of the Metropolitan Museum of Art, Rogers Fund, 1941 (41.162.29)

Page 30, ICARE (ICARUS) *by Henri Matisse (1869–1954), plate 8 from* Jazz. *Paris, published by Tériade, 1947.*
 Courtesy of the Metropolitan Museum of Art, gift of Lila Acheson Wallace, 1983 (1983.1009)

Page 32, JOVE/ZEUS *by Sabatelli, ceiling fresco, the Hall of the Iliad*
 Courtesy of the Galleria Paletina, Florence
  Photo: Scala/Art Resource, NY

Page 34, HADES *(ca. 4th century B.C.), Greek krater*
 Courtesy of the Thessalonike Museum
  Photo: Art Resource, NY

Page 36, AUTUMN *by Leon Spillaert (1881–1946), watercolor and wash*
 Courtesy of a private collection
  Photo: Giraudon/Art Resource, NY

Page 39, GIRL WITH PIGEONS *(ca. 455–450 B.C.), Greek grave relief from the island of Paros, Parian marble (h. 31 1/2" w. 15 3/8")*
 Courtesy of the Metropolitan Museum of Art, Fletcher Fund, 1927 (27.45)

Page 42, SEATED OLD MAN WITH RIGHT ARM UPRAISED *by Giovanni Francesco Barbieri Guercino (1591–1666), red chalk on blue paper (h. 23.3 cm w. 31.7 cm)*
 Courtesy of the Metropolitan Museum of Art, Rogers Fund, 1970 (1970.168)

Page 44, CIRCE *by Gustav Moreau (1826–98), oil on canvas*
 Courtesy of the Museé Gustav Moreau, Paris
  Photo: Giraudon/Art Resource, NY

Page 47, SOLDIERS HOMECOMING TO THE TYRANNY OF GENETIC ENGINEERS *(1989) by Emilio Cruz, oil on canvas (5' × 6')*
 Courtesy of the artist

Page 48, WHINING WOMAN *by Pablo Picasso (1881–1973), pen, ink, and wash on paper*
  Photo: Marburg/Art Resource, NY

Page 50, THE EMPEROR AUGUSTUS *(ca. 1st century A.D.), Roman sardonyx cameo*
    Courtesy of the British Museum, London
        Photo: Art Resource, NY

Page 52, THE JUDGMENT OF SOLOMON *(ca. A.D. 50), fresco from Pompeii*
    Courtesy of the National Museum, Naples
        Photo: Scala/Art Resource, NY

Page 54, *Detail from* PRIMAVERA *by Sandro Botticelli (1445–1510)*
    Courtesy of the Uffizi Gallery, Florence
        Photo: Scala/Art Resource, NY

Page 58, MYTHOLOGICAL SCENE *by Polidoro da Caravaggio (ca. 1500–1543)*
    Courtesy of the Metropolitan Museum of Art, Robert Lehman Collection, 1975
    (1975.1.408)

Page 63, DEATH'S DAY *(1985) by Emilio Cruz, oil and pastel on paper (30" × 39")*
    Courtesy of the artist

Page 65, LE HIBOU *by Raoul Dufy (1877–1953), woodblock illustration from* Le Bestiaire
ou Cortège d'Orphée *by Apollinaire (published in 1911 by Deplanche, Paris; reprint ©
1977 The Metropolitan Museum of Art)*
    Courtesy of the Metropolitan Museum of Art, Harris Brisbane Dick Fund, 1926
    (26.92.30)

Page 66, ATHENA VARVAKEION *(ca. 2nd century A.D.), copy of the* Athena Parthenos di
Phidia, *marble (approx. life-size)*
    Courtesy of the National Museum, Athens
        Photo: Nimatallah/Art Resource, NY

Page 69, HARPIES ON A ROCKY BEACH *(1984) by Earl Staley, acrylic on paper (22 1/4" ×
30 1/4")*
    Courtesy of the artist and the Ruth Siegel Gallery, NY

Page 70, SKETCH OF A MAN *by Leonardo da Vinci (1452–1519), pen and ink on paper*
        Photo: Scala/Art Resource, NY

Page 73, STUDY OF A BEAR WALKING *by Leonardo da Vinci, silverpoint on light buff prepared
paper (4 1/16" × 5 1/4")*
    Courtesy of the Metropolitan Museum of Art, Robert Lehman Collection, 1975
    (1975.1.369)

Page 76, COIN FROM SYRACUSE *(ca. 1st century A.D.)*
    Courtesy of the Museum of Archaeology, Syracuse
        Photo: Scala/Art Resource

Page 80, ULYSSES ON CIRCE'S ISLAND *by Giovanni Stradano (1523–1605), oil on wood*
    Courtesy of the Palazzo Vecchio, Florence
        Photo: Scala/Art Resource, NY